DATE DUE

GAYLORD 234   PRINTED IN U. S. A.

In the Spin of Things

In the Spin of Things

of

Poetry of Motion

by
Rebecca Kai Dotlich

Illustrations by
Karen Dugan

Wordsong • Boyds Mills Press

To Steve, for the spinning of years
—R. K. D.

To all my nieces and nephews,
who are definitely in the spin of things
—K. D.

Text copyright © 2003 by Rebecca Kai Dotlich
Illustrations copyright © 2003 by Karen Dugan

Published by Wordsong
Boyds Mills Press, Inc.
A Highlights Company
815 Church Street
Honesdale, Pennsylvania 18431
Printed in China

Publisher Cataloging-in-Publication Data (U.S.)

Dotlich, Rebecca Kai.
In the spin of things : poetry of motion / by Rebecca Kai Dotlich ;
illustrations by Karen Dugan.—1st ed.
[32] p. : col. ill. ; cm.
Summary: Original poems about spinning objects both natural and man-made,
including leaves, wind, a carousel, and a washing machine.
ISBN 1-56397-145-3
1. Poetry. 2. Motion—Poetry. I. Dugan, Karen. II. Title.
811.54 21 AC CIP 2003
2002108406

First edition, 2003
The text of this book is set in 13-point Stone Serif.

Visit our Web site at www.boydsmillspress.com

10 9 8 7 6 5 4 3 2 1

CONTENTS

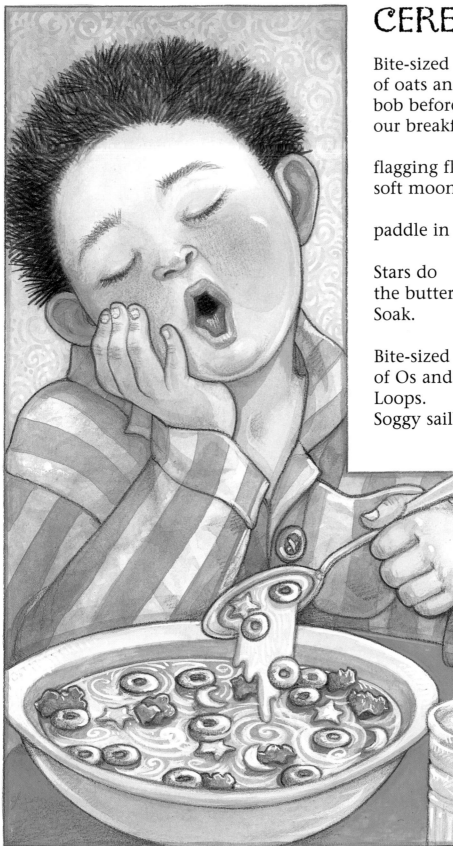

CEREAL

Bite-sized bits
of oats and Os
bob before
our breakfast nose,

flagging flakes,
soft moons

paddle in spoons.

Stars do
the butterfly stroke.
Soak.

Bite-sized bits
of Os and oats.
Loops.
Soggy sailboats.

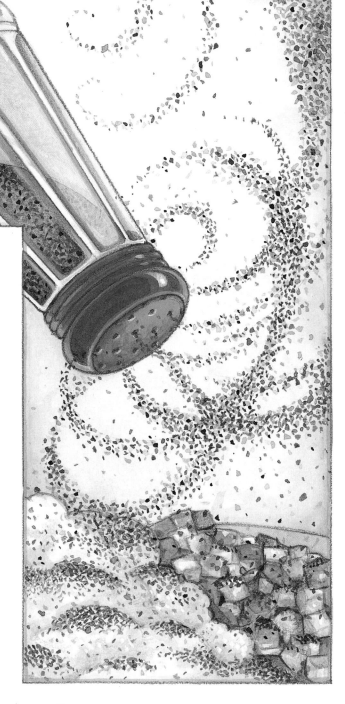

PEPPER SHAKER

Packed with a million
midnight spots;
dots of **pepper**
    piled
upon **pepper**.
Turn upside down,
shake it on
hot hash browns,
sprinkle it
on scrambled eggs.
Set the shaker
on its base,
hot dots settle
into place,
inside
its **peppered**
palace.

WINDSHIELD WIPERS

Squish, squish,
squeegy-squish,
tossing rain
side   to   side;
squish, squish,
squeegy-squish,
flap, flap,
puddle glide.
Slosh, slosh,
sloshing wash,
plish, plish,
tidal toss.
Squeegy-squish,
squish, squish, sway . . .

a perfect windshield
wiper day.

AUTUMN LEAVES

gather in gutters,
pile on walks,
tumble
        from the tips
of toes,
crunching
fall *hellos*
to back-to-school feet.

JUMP ROPE

S w i n g s
       up,
whirls around,
brushes ground
beneath quick feet.
Sweeps walks,
slap, slip,
double Dutch,
scissor skip.
Flip, flap,
LOOPS around,
slip, slap,
swoops down.
Slides and swirls,
twirls and twists,
song for a jump rope
sounds like this:
Tiger leap,
spider spin,
your turn next,
jump on in!

PENCIL SHARPENER

WHIRS
in the middle,
gnaws
and nibbles,
whittles and whirs,
whittles and whirs
with cravings
for shavings
of pencil,
the pencil,
it spins
in the middle,
the middle,
      the middle,
until
it is full,
until it is fed
with peelings
of pencils . . .
the BREAKFAST
OF LEAD.

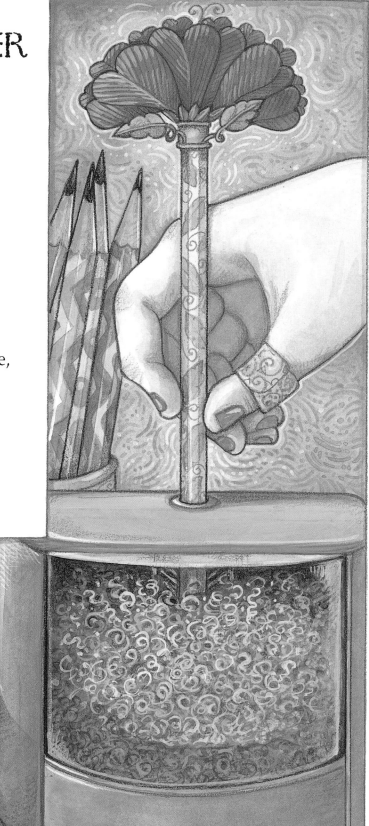

SCISSORS

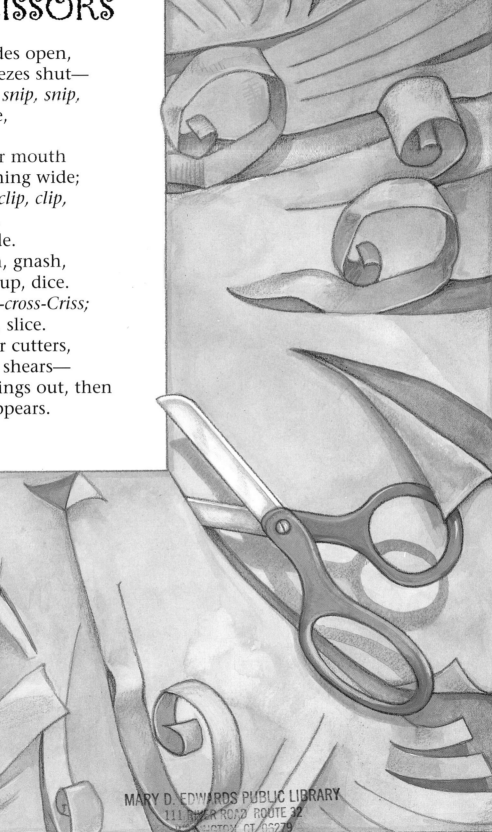

X slides open,
squeezes shut—
snip, snip, snip,
carve,
cut.
Silver mouth
yawning wide;
clip, clip, clip,
split,
divide.
Slash, gnash,
dice up, dice.
Criss-cross-Criss;
slice, slice.
Paper cutters,
steel shears—
X swings out, then
disappears.

RUBBER BAND

Strrrrrrr—etch
fling, ping!
Tug,
     twang.
Sprrrrrr—ing.
Sting.
Twist. Rap.
   SLAP.

CLASSROOM GLOBE

Spinning, spinning,
round
and round,
a swirl of blue,
a whirl of brown;
mountain ranges,
oceans,
lakes,
islands,
foreign countries,
states.

Spinning, spinning,
stop!
Then linger.
Trace the earth
beneath
one finger.

Spinning, spinning,
round
and round,
a swirl of blue,
a whirl of brown.

Spinning, spinning,
round
and round.

ICE CUBES

Drop,
plop,
one at a time,

hear their crackling,
clinking chime.

Drop three more,
plop,
   plop,
      plop,
watch them bounce
and belly flop,

mixing, scrambling,
changing places—
chilly cubes,
frozen faces

bobbing all
around the side,
frosty romping,
dip
   and dive,

around the rim
they swirl,
swim,
melting smaller,
smallest, small,
until they are not
there
at

all.

WATERFALLS

come spilling
bluer
    than blue;
splashing
cool buckets
of giant's tears
over tops of mountains
into the gurgling laps
of rivers.

HELICOPTER

Sways backward.
Swerves sideways.
Stays low. Bravo!
Hovers, hops,
stops midair.
Twirls there
in a spot of sky.
Gollywopper,
Pinwheel Popper,
Summit King;
paddle blades whirl
in the spin of things.
Old Gazelle,
Ballet Bell,
Island Hopper;
have you ever
seen a chopper
dangling over
ragged mountain,
raging river . . .
shiver!

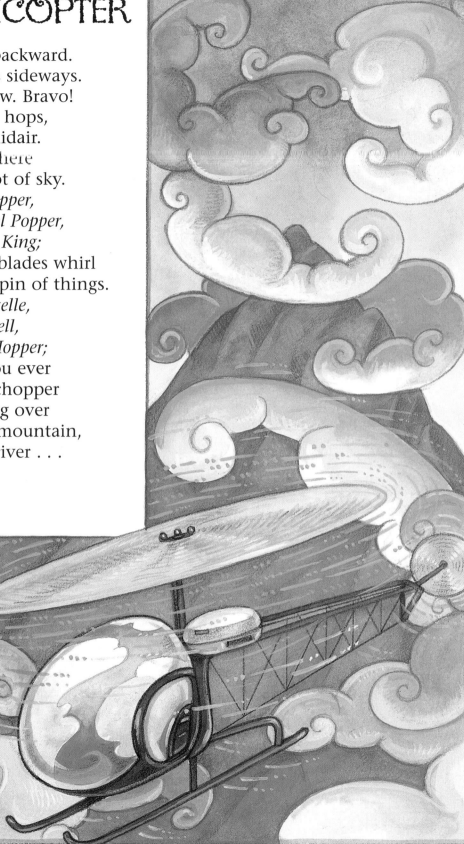

ODE TO THE WASHING MACHINE

Here's to your spin; your soapsud song—
your rumble and whirl and twirl along

        swish swish swish
swirl and spin,
a tub of tumbling safety pins

and jeans and socks
        and nickels that knock
their silver song in the whirling drum
of your belly.

Twist, tub, twist,
        do the twist,
give the socks a soapy kiss;
scrub our jeans good and clean,
yellow the yellows, green-up the greens.

        Bub bub bubble
bubble along . . .
here's to your spin, your soapsud song.

LAWN MOWER

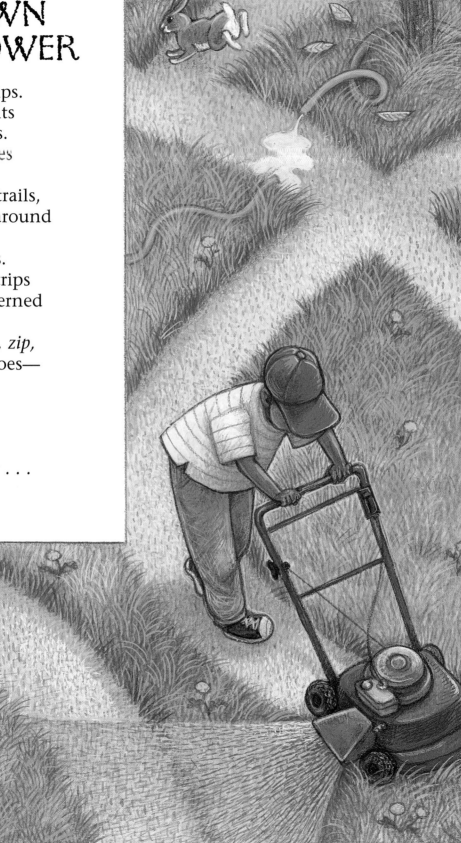

Clips tips.
Spits bits
of grass.
Scribbles
paths,
forges trails,
snails around
a maze
of trees.
Snips strips
in patterned
rows,
zip, zip, zip,
zip it goes—
clips
tips,
sprays
bits,
sputters . . .

spits.

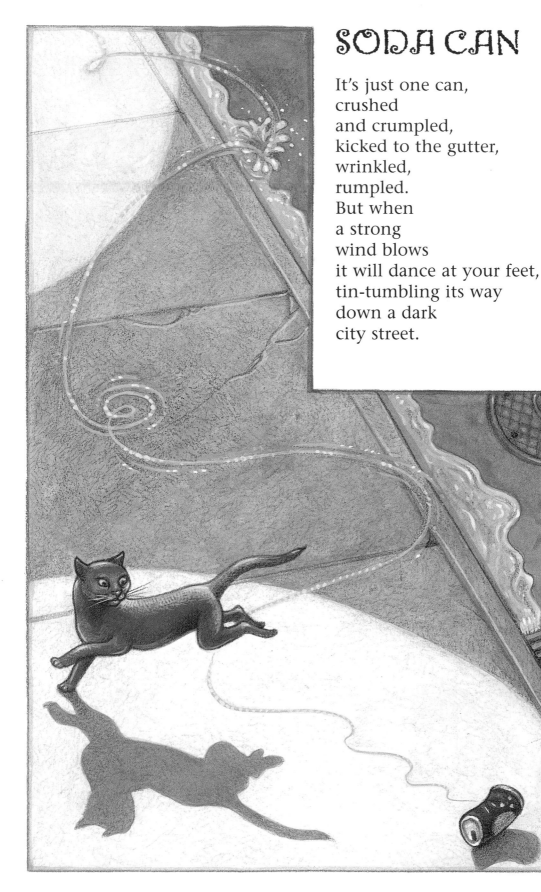

SODA CAN

It's just one can,
crushed
and crumpled,
kicked to the gutter,
wrinkled,
rumpled.
But when
a strong
wind blows
it will dance at your feet,
tin-tumbling its way
down a dark
city street.

LADY WIND

Watch
the growing
little-girl breeze
wave her hands
swoosh, swoosh,
around
and in between
the pear, the elm,
the sycamore tree;
howling wild
wind words
to squirrels,
papa birds, and bugs—
shake, shake, shaking
limb and leaf.
Watch, *swoosh*—
the grown-up breeze!
Just yesterday
she was small and warm;
today she is
a quarreling storm.

WIND CHIMES

Clanging
sea secrets
to the wind,
tin ballerinas
on a tangle
of string
sing
their bittersweet
songs;
sweet voices
of chattering ghosts.

PUPPETS

These jointed hips,
these wobbly knees
move to the music
of make-believe;
they'd ask you to dance
if only they could,
but they (alas) are made
of wood.

CAROUSEL

On thin golden poles
gliding up, sliding down,
a kingdom of horses
goes spinning around.

Jumper, Brown Beauty,
Dark Thunder, Sir Snow,
a medley of ponies
parade in a row.

Settled in saddles,
their riders hold on
to reins of soft leather
while circling along

on chestnut or charcoal,
on sleek Arctic white,
on silver they gallop
in place day and night.

Such spinning is magic,
(to dream as you sail)
with lavender saddle
and ebony tail,

whirling to music
in moonlight, spellbound,
galloping, galloping,
merrily go round.

KITCHEN BROOM

Standing
in a corner,
leaning on the wall,
this stiff and sturdy
straight and tall
sweeping soldier
stands on call;
begins his *swooshing*
job by heart
(crumb of cookie falls apart);

. . . sweep to the left,
. . . sweep to the right,

dance away,
dance away
crumbs tonight.

THE IRONING HOUR

Sprinkle.
Unwrinkle.
Smooth.
Remove
another wrinkle.
Steam seam.
Glide up.
Slide down.
Ride around
the buttons.
Time to learn.
Your turn.
Dad's shirt.
Pillowcase.
Watch the lace.
Erase
another wrinkle.
Time to learn.
Your turn.
Don't burn.
Hold tight.
That's right.
Smooth flat.
Like that.
Don't tug.
Unplug.

ROLLER COASTER

C
R
A
W
L
S L O W and steady,
hold on,
get ready,
oh so
slow it climbs,
   turtling,
       turtling,
         turtling up,
you know the drill
of the thrill:
how it creeps,
   crawls,
stalls
for a spell—
an almost-stop
on top—
   then *WHOOOSSSHHH,*

d
o
w
n
   (into) the dip,
back up,
around,
hugging
the armored
humpback track;
claketyclaketyclaketyclack.

CANDLE FLAME

Watch carefully
the candle
flame;
its yellow dance,
its curvy wave . . .
an oven on
one leg of wick.
High above we shape
our lips into an **O**, then blow
its fire dance away,
then say good night
to butter-bright
and candlelight.